That Seeing, They May Believe

52 Children's Object Lessons

Kenneth Mortonson

CSS Publishing Company, Inc.
Lima, Ohio

THAT SEEING, THEY MAY BELIEVE

Library of Congress Cataloging-in-Publication Data

Mortonson, Kenneth A., 1927-
    That seeing, they may believe : children's object lessons / by Kenneth A. Mortonson.
        p   c.m
    Includes index.
    ISBN 1-55672-652-5
    1. Children's sermons. 2. Object-teaching. 3. Christian education — Teaching methods. 4. Christian education — Home training. 5. Christian education of children. I. Title.
BV4315.M66   1993
252'.53—dc20   **8-9 9**   93-18007
                                                                      CIP

9352 / ISBN 1-55673-652-5   PRINTED IN U.S.A.

This book is dedicated to my ten grandchildren who represent the next generation of Christians:

Michael and Nikolaus Wilim
Christopher and Cathleen Mortonson
Eric, Adam, Aaron and Ryan Kline
Michael and Andrew Mortonson

Table Of Contents

Preface

By James W. Cox
Victor and Louise Lester Professor of Christian Preaching
The Southern Baptist Theological Seminary
Louisville, Kentucky

Everybody loves a story. This is a truism that no one would like to debate. Why do we love a story? It is concrete; it is about people; it has something in it that is important to someone. The same can be said about an object lesson, though the dynamics may be a bit subtler. Also, a dialogue without a story or an object lesson can function as a story when the child who is engaged in the dialogue becomes a character in the discussion, even though he or she says not a word.

To the embarrassment of some pastors, their congregations love and listen to their children's sermons more than their "adult" sermons. However, this does not mean that the grownups are simply being entertained and not edified. These little stories, object lessons, and dialogues can convey an enormous freight of Christian truth.

In addition, they make possible the establishing and deepening of a relationship between the person speaking and the people listening. In fact, one graduate student, writing a master's thesis on children's sermons, argued that this is the main purpose of such sermons.

Certainly this agrees with Phillips Brooks' oft-quoted definition of preaching, as "truth through personality." The unspoken message that accompanies the children's sermon in a regular service of worship is manifold. It says: You are important, too. You are loved. Your minister is "people" also and your friend.

Kenneth Mortonson is sensitive to the requirements of a children's sermon at every point. I saw his work first in the bi-monthly journal *Preaching* and liked what I read. Since then I have used his exemplary work in *The Minister's Manual,*

7

which I edit for Harper/Collins annually. His children's sermons are characterized by imagination, clarity, variety, interest-
ingness and faithfulness to the intent of Holy Scripture. The
sermons in this book can be used in different contexts "as is,"
as starters for speakers' own thought processes, or for sermon
illustrations. It is a valuable contribution to a special homi-
letical art.

Introduction

This book is dedicated to all who seek to teach the Christian faith. It is for parents, preachers, teachers and anyone else who desires to present Christian ideas to this present generation.

There are several ways in which the thoughts presented here may be utilized. One way is to use the suggested symbols and read the material directly from the printed page. Another way is to take the material on these pages as a guide; and then adapt them to materials you have on hand and to the person or people to whom you seek to communicate the idea. It is also my hope that the experience of using this book will open the reader's eyes to the many symbols in our world that can be used to illustrate God's truths.

The material presented here is primarily for use in the worship or church school setting. However, it is my sincere hope that the thoughts will also be used by parents in the context of the home. If the Christian faith is not expressed in the daily activities and materials of the home, then what happens in the church will have little lasting effect. Parents need to prepare themselves for the all-important task of training the child in the way he or she should go in the belief that children properly trained will not depart from that training when they mature in the faith. In the words of Proverbs 22:6, "Train up a child in the way he should go, and when he is old he will not depart from it."

There are 52 illustrations within this book. This will give the reader a year's supply of teaching material for weekly use in home or church. Included in that number are illustrations geared to special days or seasons. For example, "Symbols Of Thanksgiving — Stone And Rope" is for the Sunday before Thanksgiving. However, many of the special day sermonettes can be adapted for use at other times. At the end of the book, you will find an index by subject matter.

I would recommend that the parent who desires to use this material in the home should read through the book and note the suggestions of possible times when the setting may be right for teaching. Some of the conditions can be worked into your weekly routine. Others will arise out of special occasions. Some conditions will appear spontaneously. The important point is to be alert to those times when your child will be most receptive to the message of the illustrations.

Remember: "The earth is the Lord's and the fulness thereof, the world and those who dwell therein." (Psalm 24:1)

Kenneth A. Mortonson
Macomb, Illinois

Lo, I Am With You Always

Purpose: To help understand how Jesus influences our lives.

Materials: A ping pong ball or any type of small light plastic ball. A vacuum cleaner with a hose attachment and the ability to reverse the air flow so that the air is blown out rather than sucked in.

Special Preparation: Practice this procedure before you attempt to do it before other people. Be sure the air is flowing out of the tube. Hold the hose of the vacuum cleaner in an upright position so that the air is blowing straight up. Place the ball in the flow of air. It should float there. The ball can be moved through the air by slowly moving the hose from one side to another.

Lesson: One of the promises Jesus made to his disciples was, "Lo, I am with you always." (Matthew 28:20) Since we cannot actually see Jesus, it is hard for most people to understand how he keeps this promise. One of the ways Jesus shows us that he is always with us is by what he does to our lives. We see what happens, we feel something, but we cannot actually see him.

By making the air flow the other way through this vacuum cleaner, we learn how we can see and feel something even though we cannot see the force itself. *(Turn on the machine and place the ball in the air stream.)*

11

Another interesting feature of this force is that as you move it the object caught in its power moves with it. Jesus said, "Take my yoke upon you, and learn from me . . . ." (Matthew 11:29) When we are joined to our Lord, his power is seen in our lives. He guides us as we learn from him. His effect upon us shows us that he is with us. As we move through life with Jesus, we are attached to him by an unseen force that is always with us.

Possible Times To Use This Illustration In The Home:
- When children have been playing ping pong, or some other game that uses a small ball.
- During the time of cleaning the house.
- When a child questions why we cannot see the risen Lord.

What Shall We Be?

Purpose: To stress the importance of what a child learns in the early years.

Materials: Plaster of Paris, rubber mold and an object made from the mold.

Lesson: Maybe you have had an opportunity to take some plaster of Paris and a mold like this and make a toy. To do so, you begin with a certain amount of water and then you add enough of this white powder to make a thick paste. After you have stirred your mixture, you pour it into the mold and set it aside to wait for it to harden. When it is hard, you remove the rubber mold and you have your toy.

In a way, this process reminds us of your life. We will let the water represent you as a newborn child. You entered the world knowing very little and acting just like all other babies. But then, you began to learn certain things. The things you learned were like the adding of plaster of Paris to the water. Now, you are still learning new things. During all this time, you live in a special place. Your home and community are like the rubber mold. It is supporting you as you grow up. Some day, if all goes well, when the time is right, the mold can be removed and you will end up as a person who is unique among all people. Some day you will be old enough to move into your own home and community.

This illustration says many things, but let me point out just two of them. First, it says to you, "The things you learn now are very important. They will determine what you will be like in later years. Therefore, take advantage of your opportunities to learn so that you will have all you need when you grow up. Remember also that religious training is a very important part of what you need to know for life. The best time to obtain it is now while you are young."

To the parents and other adults, this illustration says, "Make sure that the example of your home and community provides these young children with the best shaped mold or pattern that you can construct. Once they leave your environment there is little you can do to prepare them for life."

Possible Times To Use This Illustration In The Home:
- When making a repair on the house, thus giving thought to the importance of the home improvement.
- When making something in the craft line.
- When something unusual happens in the community, thus providing the opportunity for a conversation about the importance of environment.

Pieces Of Paper

Purpose: Understanding values.

Materials: Several pieces of paper of different colors, cut to the size of a dollar bill. A one dollar bill.

Lesson: After you have had a chance to look at these pieces of paper, I want you to tell me which one you would like to have. Let's take a vote. If you could have one of these pieces of paper, how many would take this one? *(Hold up the dollar bill.)* I wonder why all (or most) of you chose the dollar bill? It's just a piece of paper like the others. It may look nicer than the others, since it has some printing on it; but if you wanted some paper to draw on, would you still take the dollar bill? *(Yes, because then you could buy some plain paper to use.)*

Of all the pieces of paper here, only the dollar bill has value, for it stands for something greater than the paper upon which it is printed. Printed on this paper are the words, "Federal Reserve Note. This note is legal tender for all debts." That means that you can use this piece of paper to buy something that costs one dollar.

Paper money is a symbol, an instrument of exchange. Instead of carrying silver or gold around with us, we carry this lighter paper.

The use of money is also a symbolic thing. What we use it for shows what we think is of value in life. Often the value of something is in what it stands for rather than in the thing itself. For example, a picture drawn by a little child has little monetary value, but it can be very valuable to the parents who receive it. For them, a part of their child's life went into the drawing of that picture and it shows the way the child is developing and, therefore, it is very valuable to the parents.

There is one other thing I would like you to notice about the dollar bill. On each bill there is a different number. Each bill is unique as well as precious. The same is true of you in God's eyes. You are unique and precious to him. As you live your life, as God wants you to live, your true value will be seen by everyone.

Possible Times To Use This Illustration In The Home:

- When there is need to talk about the value of things. It is not what we have but how we use what we have that is important.
- When the child has been spending too much money on frivolous things.

Putting God In His Place

Purpose: To show the importance of keeping God at the center of life.

Materials: A small toy car with a friction motor. Several large cardboard disks, glued together. A pencil. Drill a hole, the diameter of the pencil, through the center of the disk; and drill another hole about one inch off the center.

Lesson: By just looking at this toy car, you cannot tell what kind it is; but when I spin the wheels, the sound tells you that this is a special kind of car. Once you have the wheels turning fast, they will continue to run for quite a while. The reason for this is that within the car are several other wheels. Some of these wheels have what we call teeth. They are gears. The teeth of one wheel mesh with the teeth of another wheel and, as the first wheel turns, it makes the second one go around.

Now, connected to all of this, is a larger thick wheel that is called a fly wheel. Because of its size and weight, once it starts going around, it keeps going for a long time. Let me show you how it works. *(Take the cardboard disk, put the pencil through the center hole and spin the wheel.)*

One very important fact about this flywheel is that it must turn about the center. If that does not happen, then it will wobble. *(Show by placing the pencil in the off center hole and spinning the disk.)* If this was a real flywheel, and if you make it spin very fast when it is off center like this, it would break apart. In order for it to work as it should, the flywheel must be set up so that every part of the wheel rotates around the true center.

Now God wants us to be able to run smoothly in this world. *(Return the pencil to the center hole and spin the disk.)* He wants us to do what we are made to do and not wobble around or break into pieces. The only way that we can do this is to put God in his place; and his place is at the center of our lives. This means that God must become our main guide to living, and everything else must rotate around him. That is, everything must be viewed in relationship to God, for he is of first importance to us. As Jesus said, "Seek first his kingdom and his righteousness, and all these *(other)* things shall be yours as well." (Matthew 6:33) In order for God to be at the center of life, we must accept him as our Lord and Master.

Possible Times To Use This Illustration In The Home:
- When a child is playing with a toy car.
- When a child would rather do something else instead of going to your church for worship or study or Christian fellowship.
- When your child idolizes an entertainer, or when something else has become of primary importance.

Through Others Too Far Away

Purpose: To show the affect of our influence upon others.

Materials: Obtain six small objects, such as wooden spools, wooden craft beads, or plastic film containers. Tie a piece of string to each object and suspend it from a rod. Arrange the six items on the rod so that they are touching each other. When you swing the first object so that it hits the others, the last object should swing away from the group.

Lesson: It is usually not too hard to see the way our actions affect the people who are near to us. We do something nice for someone, and we see their smile or we hear the words, "thank you." But what we often forget is that what we say or do affects not only the people near to us, but also those far away; people whom we may never see.

This is the way it works, in simple terms: What we do affects someone else and their reaction affects another person, and so on. Like the wave made by a stone that is dropped into the water and spreads out farther and farther; so our words and deeds spread through others to far away places and people.

We can see how this works with this row of (whatever your objects may be). See what happens when I pull back the first one and let it strike the group. The shock of the first hit passes through the other ones and the last one swings away.

The same thing can happen in life. We do something to some one and what we do to them — good or bad — affects them; and they, in turn, affect the people who are around them. See how important it is to be careful about what you say and do. If kindness and gentle words go forth from your life, you will be an influence for good in far away places.

Possible Times To Use This Illustration In The Home:
- When your child comes home and is upset by what some-one else has done to them. Your child's unhappiness affects the whole family.
- When the family together encounters a person who is unhappy and that person did not treat you in a very pleasant way. This might happen at the check-out counter in a store.
- When your child thinks his or her attitude does not affect other people.

Seed Time

Purpose: To see death as a time of new life.

Materials: Seeds and a plant with flowers.

Lesson: Boys and girls often hear a great deal about death and, perhaps, have even seen a person die. But it isn't very often that you hear anything about the meaning of this final event in life here.

An understanding of death is given to us in the symbol of the seed. Hundreds of years ago, Paul wrote, "But someone will ask, 'How are the dead raised up? With what kind of body do they come?' You foolish man! What you sow does not come to life unless it dies. And what you sow is not the body which is to be, but a bare kernel, perhaps of wheat or of some other grain. But God gives it a body as he has chosen, and to each kind of seed its own body.'' (1 Corinthians 15:35-38)

In other words, what Paul is saying is that we take a seed and bury it in the ground and from that tiny seed there comes a new form of life. See these flowers? We must never forget that such beauty came from a tiny seed that was buried in the ground. In the words of the poet:

> "We drop a seed into the ground,
>   A tiny, shapeless thing, shriveled and dry,

And in the fullness of its time, is seen
A form of peerless beauty, robed and crowned
Beyond the pride of any earthly queen,
Instinct with loveliness, and sweet and rare.
The perfect emblem of its Master's care.
This from a shriveled seed?
Then may man hope indeed!
For man is but the seed of what he shall be,
When, in the fullness of his perfecting,
He drops the husk and cleaves his upward way
Through earth's retardings and clinging clay
Into the sunshine of God's perfect day.
No fetters then. No bonds of time or space.
But powers as ample as the boundless grace.
That suffered man and death and yet in tenderness
Set wide the door and passed Himself before
As He had promised — to prepare a place.
We know not what we shall be — only this
That we shall be made like Him, as He is."

Author — John Oxenham
(16th Century)

Possible Times To Use This Illustration In The Home:
- To help a child understand death.
- In the spring, when flowers are blooming, to plant the seed of understanding for that time when death may enter the family circle through the death of a friend or loved one.

The Light Of The World

Purpose: To show how our lives need to reflect what we believe.

Materials: A bright flashlight (or a spotlight), a mirror and a box, open at the top, in which to hide the light.

Lesson: Jesus said, "I am the light of the world; he who follows me will not walk in darkness, but will have the light of life." (John 8:12) This means more than just having a light to help us see where we are going and what we are to do. A light can also be used to guide people to a certain place when it is dark. For that to happen, the light must be seen. But sometimes the light is out of the sight of the person who needs it. When that happens, we need something to reflect the light so that it can be seen.

Let me show you what I mean. I have a bright light here, that I shall hide from view. *(Place it in the box.)* Now look up at the ceiling. *(Reflect the light up by using the mirror within the box.)* You cannot see the flashlight (or lamp) that is the source of the light, but when I reflect the light off the mirror, then it can be seen even when you are not looking in the direction of the lamp.

As we study the Bible and see what Jesus has done and taught, he shines into our life. As we pray and sing to him, we receive inspiration from him. Now, that which we have received must be seen, for we are like this mirror. We catch

23

the rays of his light and reflect them so that they may be seen by others. Many people are not looking at Jesus; they are not studying his words or seeking to follow him. But they can see a reflection of him in our life if we try to live as he would have us live. What we have received we are to share with others. In other words, we are to send out the light that has come to us.

Possible Times To Use This Illustration In The Home:
- When an older brother or sister does not set a good example.
- When using a mirror, as in the bathroom or when getting dressed.

Let Your Light Shine

Purpose: To encourage children to share.

Materials: A candle and a jar. The jar should be large enough so that it can be placed over the top of the candle when it is lighted.

Lesson: Jesus said, "Let your light so shine before men, that they may see your good works and give glory to your Father who is in heaven." (Matthew 5:16) A person's life is like a candle. The candle can be very useful in a dark room as it gives off light. It is doing what it was created to do.

Each one of you has a purpose in life. You are to live with God and with one another. You are to share your life with the world around you by doing good to others; by being kind and showing concern. In this way, you let your light shine. As soon as you stop living for others, as soon as you stop sharing what you can do and what you have with others, then you lose the purpose of life.

As I said before, this candle is like a person's life. When the wick is lighted, it gives off the light and warmth for which the candle was created. But watch what happens when I cover the flame. I am using this jar so that you can see what happens. *(Cover the flame with the jar, but do not let the jar touch the flame. Hold it there until the flame goes out.)* The candle has lost its purpose for being.

25

I hope you boys and girls will always be willing to share what you have with others. In that way, your light in life will shine brightly, to the glory of God who gave you your life for a purpose.

Possible Times To Use This Illustration In The Home:
- At the dinner table, when candles are part of the setting.
- When the children of the family have been unwilling to share things with others.
- During a time of electrical power failure, when candlelight becomes essential to the living of life at night.

The Do-It-Yourself Kit

Purpose: To encourage children to use their God-given powers.

Materials: A quart bottle with an opening a little smaller than an egg. (A glass milk bottle is ideal.) A hard-boiled egg with the shell removed. A small amount of paper. A match.

Special Preparation: (You may want to practice beforehand.) Roll or crumple up the paper so that it can be placed in the bottle. Light the paper and immediately push it into the bottle. The paper must be burning in the bottle. Immediately place the egg in the opening. Be sure that it seals the opening to the bottle. As the oxygen is consumed by the fire, the egg will be sucked into the bottle in one piece.

Lesson: I have a problem. I want to get this egg into this bottle. But as you can see, the egg is bigger than the opening. If I push the egg it will crumble before I can force it in.

Now, there is a way to get the egg into the bottle in one piece. Let me show you. I will put a small fire into the bottle and place the egg on top, and then wait. *(Do so. Wait until the egg is drawn into the bottle and then continue.)* Now, don't ever try this on your own. You should never play with fire. Fire is a force that can destroy things.

Today, I used the energy of the fire to help me solve my problem. Very often, in life, we have problems that have to be faced. Many of our problems can be solved with the help of other people. But sometimes we find that we have a problem that no one can solve for us. We must do it ourselves. It is then that we must use our own inner energies and the power of the Spirit of God that is within us. God has given each person a mind and willpower and common sense which we are to use to help solve the problems of life. He has put these powers within us just as the flame was put into the bottle. We all need to use these special powers that God has given each one of us.

Possible Times To Use This Illustration In The Home:
- At a party or some other time when you wish to entertain a group of children with a trick. *(You should speak to your child about the lesson after the party is over.)*
- At a time when your child is having difficulty solving a personal problem, to help him or her get a new perspective on their own God-given powers; and to increase self-confidence.

Keep Spinning

Purpose: To show our need for regular worship and study; and to see our need to put into practice what we have learned from God.

Materials: A piece of cardboard and a piece of string, about four feet long.

Special Preparation: Draw a five or six inch circle on the piece of cardboard and cut out the disk. Punch two small holes in the disk, about one-eighth of an inch on either side of the center of the circle. Loop the string through these two holes and tie the ends together. Hold the knot in one hand and the looped end in the other. Twirl the disk around several times and then repeatedly pull the string and release slightly in order to keep the disk twirling. Practice so that you can get the right rhythm to keep the cardboard disk spinning.

Lesson: Maybe you have played with a toy like this at some time. It is a simple toy that you can make. What you try to do with this toy is to keep the disk rotating, once it has been started, by twisting and pulling the string at the right time. As long as you keep pulling and releasing, the disk will continue to spin; if you maintain the right rhythm.

Here we see a simple principle that we need to apply to the Christian life. To keep the cardboard disk spinning, two things must be done. You must pull at the right time and then you must slightly release that pull, at the right time.

This pattern can also have meaning for our Christian life. We also need two things. First of all, we need to remember that our religion is God-given, not man-made. God speaks to us, God motivates us, God guides us. This he does through the study of his word, and through our worship of him. These are the things that help us live an active Christian life. These are things that energize our life like the pull on the string that rotates our disk.

Now, remember, to keep the disk spinning, one pull was not enough. Likewise, to worship now and then, to study only once in a while, is not enough to keep the Christian life working as it should. The rhythm that is needed in life is to gather regularly for worship and study, and then to take what we have learned and live by it.

Living by what we believe is the second thing that is needed to keep the Christian life going strong. We take what we have received from God and we return it to the world in which we live. We love others, because God first loved us. We forgive others because we know that God has forgiven us. We help others with the difficult things they must do because God has helped us in life. We take the power that has been given to us in worship and study, and we release it into our world. But, then after we have done that, we must return to worship and study to be strengthened and nurtured again. This give and take is what will keep your Christian life moving, as with the spinning disk.

Possible Times To Use This Illustration In The Home:
- On that day when your child doesn't know what to do. Let him or her make this toy and while it is being used in play, you might raise the subject of how we receive from others and then we must give of ourselves to others. This give and take is part of the rhythm of true life.
- When a child thinks only in terms of receiving things and needs to think about giving also.

30

The Lightning And The Current

Purpose: To stress our need of Jesus to show us how to do good things.

Materials: An electric lamp and a piece of white paper cut to represent a bolt of lightning.

Lesson: These two objects remind us of something that we see and use often. Every time we have a thunderstorm, we see the powerful destructive stabs of lightning ripping through the wet air. Most of the time, we look out upon the storm from a warm, well-lighted house where we are safe from the storm.

Now, the lights in our home and the lightning in the storm are charged with the same kind of power, namely, electricity. In one form, it is dangerous and destructive. In the other form, it is a quiet and steady current that makes it safe for us to walk around at night.

We also have great powers within us; powers that can be used for good or evil. We have the power to think, to move, to speak and to act. All these powers have been given to us by God. With these powers we have also received the responsibility to use them in a proper way.

In the Christian faith, we believe that no one can learn the proper use of these God-given powers alone. Therefore, we turn to Jesus for the perfect example of what it means to use the gifts of God as they were intended to be used. When Jesus acted, miracles were performed; and there is no greater miracle than the act of kindness and compassion. When Jesus spoke, people replied, "No man ever spoke like this man!" (John 7:46) for he spoke the truth. As we follow Jesus, we too shall learn how to use our God-given powers for good instead of evil. Jesus said, "I am the way, and the truth, and the life; no one comes to the Father, but by me." (John 14:6) Every life, regardless of age or condition, has great powers for good within it, if that life is lived under God's direction.

Possible Times To Use This Illustration In The Home:
- During a thunderstorm.
- When a child has used his abilities in a wrong way; perhaps hurting someone or destroying something.
- When a child thinks that his or her abilities are small and unimportant. (The lamp is more useful than the powerful bolt of lightning.)

Inner Warmth

Purpose: Learning to express love.

Materials: A pop bottle, a balloon and a candle.

Special Preparation: Place the neck of the balloon over the neck of the pop bottle. Hold the bottle over the flame of the candle until the air in the bottle is expanded by the heat and it begins to inflate the balloon. Practice to see how long it takes before the balloon begins to show signs of being inflated. Try to use a warm bottle.

Lesson: This morning I want to show you what happens when the air in this bottle is heated. Watch the balloon. The heat will cause the air to expand and you will see that expanded air enter the balloon.

In a way, this represents the Christian life. We are like the bottle. God's love, which is warm and wonderful, is like the flame. When God's love comes into our life it gives us what we call ''abundant life.''

However, we may not see that abundant life right away. It often takes time before we can see or feel the influence of God's love. Therefore, we need patience and we need to continue our exposure to God's love by studying his word and believing his promises. When we truly believe that God loves us it will be experienced within our life. We will be happy, for people are always happy when they know they are loved; and this happiness will be seen.

When we have felt the love of God and we realize how wonderful he has been to us and what he means to us, then we will want to share that love with others. Like the warm air in the bottle, God's love within us will warm our heart and it will expand, so to speak; then the result of that expansion will be seen. We sometimes say that a generous person is one who has a big heart.

In the letter of John, we are reminded, "We love, because he (God) first loved us." (1 John 4:19) John also wrote, "Beloved, let us love one another; for love is of God, and he who loves is born of God and knows God." (1 John 4:7) We are to be kind and courteous and helpful, not only to our parents, but to our brother and sister; and to all we meet. Let the strong, warm, steady love of God fill your life to overflowing. Then let that fullness be seen.

Possible Times To Use This Illustration In The Home:
- When there is a lack of expression of love between members of the family. If we truly accept the love others have for us, then by the very nature of love, its warmth will be shared with others.
- When an older child wants to stop attending church school. If we are to maintain the spirit of love within us, then we need to keep that warm flame burning. The study of God's word is one of the major ways of remembering what God has done for us.

Know Your Limitations

Purpose: Learning to live with our limitations.

Materials: A balloon.

Lesson: Most children, at one time or another, have come to a parent with a balloon and asked, "Please blow this up for me." Then they would stand back and watch — *(begin to blow up the balloon)* — while Mom or Dad blew, and blew, and blew. *(While you talk continue to blow up the balloon.)* And the balloon would get bigger, ... and bigger, ... and bigger, ... until ... BANG! *(If the balloon does not burst from the air you have put into it by this time, use a small pin to burst it.)*

Now, you knew that this balloon would burst sooner or later if I continued to force air into it. You knew that there was a limit to the amount of air that this balloon could hold. I knew it too, but I went beyond the limit.

There are two lessons that we can learn from this. The first lesson is that we, like the balloon, have limitations; and wise is the person who knows his or her limitations and is guided in life by them. For example, some children try to do things that they see their parents doing, like drive a car or light a match. They forget that they have not learned how to drive or how to use a lighted match in the right way. Because they are still young, limitations are often placed upon them to protect them. Adults too must learn this truth. There is a limit to what we can endure, what we can do and what we can know. We must live with our limitations, whatever they might be.

The second lesson is this. Just as we know that this balloon would burst, we must be aware of the limitations of others and be guided by that information. We often expect too much from another person simply because we will not face this truth. Many parents have been disappointed because they expected too much from their child. Many children lose respect for their parents when they do not measure up to expectations. The problem may be caused by having set the expectations too high.

Remember, a balloon filled with air is fun to have; but one that has been pushed to the breaking point is good for nothing once it has burst. Live to the fullest, but also recognize and accept the limitations life has placed upon you and others.

Possible Times To Use This Illustration In The Home:
- When a child becomes involved in too many activities.
- When someone in the family expects too much of self or others.
- When someone fails to measure up to what has been expected of that person.

Learning From Riddles

Purpose: Learning to take care of ourselves.

Materials: None needed, except the riddles in the lesson.

Lesson: I think that most children like riddles. Maybe you have heard these and you know the answers. As I ask each riddle, I want you to answer them in your mind, and then we will see if you were right.

What has eyes but cannot see? (A potato)

What has legs, but cannot walk? (A chair or table)

What has a tongue, but cannot talk? (A shoe)

How many of you knew some or all of the answers?

These items, and many others that I could name, have parts that are called by the same names as parts of our body. But God has made our parts more wonderful and useful. With our eyes, for example, we can look out on all the beauty around us. From what we see, we know that God must be wonderful, for he has made such a wonderful world in nature.

Our legs do more than hold us up. We can move them and have them carry us about from one place to another. We often do not appreciate how wonderfully God has made us until something happens and we find that we cannot use what he has given to us. Just think of all the things you would miss if you could not walk or see or hear or speak. Never take these wonderful gifts for granted! Thank God for them and use them wisely. Learn to take good care of yourself.

Possible Times To Use This Illustration In The Home:
- When your child comes home with a new riddle.
- When a child is sick because of improper personal care.
- When the attitude of the child indicates that he or she thinks that material things are more important than people.

The Sawhorse

Purpose: To show that even simple things can be used to serve God.

Materials: A real or toy sawhorse.

Lesson: Do you know what this is? It is a sawhorse and it is used by people who want to cut wood. The sawhorse holds the wood up high so that it can be easily cut. A number of years ago, a man who lived in Port Hope, Canada, used a sawhorse to serve God and his fellow man. His name was Joseph Scriven. He was born in Ireland; but he moved to Canada when he was a young man. The story is told of him that the death of a young lady he was going to marry, on the night before their wedding, caused him to turn to his father for comfort and reassurance. Some time later, he wrote a poem to share his experience with others, he wrote a poem to share his experience with others. We can hear that poem when we sing a hymn that is a favorite of many people. It is the hymn, "What A Friend We Have In Jesus."

After Joseph found peace in the life and words of Jesus, he tried to live his faith by helping people who were in need. This is where the sawhorse comes in. One day, for example, Joseph Scriven was seen on the street of his town dressed in working clothes and carrying his sawhorse. He was on his way to help a needy neighbor. Two men passed by him. One was a stranger to the community, and he asked his friend about the man with the sawhorse. He was looking for someone whom he could hire to cut some wood.

"Oh," said the other man, "that is Mr. Scriven. I'm afraid that he wouldn't work for you because you are able to pay for the work. Mr. Scriven saws wood only for the poor widows and sick people."

Today, near Rice Lake in Canada, there is a monument that has been built by the people of his community to the memory of Joseph Scriven. It stands as a constant reminder that a man inspired by the life and teachings of Jesus can use even the simplest things in life — like a sawhorse — to bring honor and glory to God and to show concern for one's neighbors.

Possible Times To Use This Illustration In The Home:
- When a sawhorse is being used, or you use firewood in your fireplace.
- When there is a sick or needy neighbor and there is something you and your children can do to help.
- When a child feels inferior because of small talents or limited materials with which to work.

Wave The Flags

Purpose: To think about what it means to say, "One nation under God."

Materials: An American flag with gold trim.

Lesson: Today we are going to look at the American flag and see what symbols we can find here and what they might mean to us as Christians.

The stars remind us of shining and the blue makes us think of the sky or heaven. These two symbols together remind us that many people in our country want us to be a nation under God. Jesus told us to let our light shine before people, or we can say, before nations so that they may see our good works and give praise to our Father who is in heaven.

The gold trim reminds us of beauty and abundance and wealth. We have a beautiful nation and the abundance of many things. This abundance, in part, has come from putting Christian principles into practice. Jesus said, "I came that they may have life and have it abundantly." (John 10:10) However, let us never forget that with the abundance comes greater responsibility, for Jesus also said, "Every one to whom much is given, of him will much be required." (Luke 12:48)

Now, the abundance of things is not necessarily the same as an abundant life. True living comes from following Jesus. How do we find true life in Jesus? First, we see his sinless life, his perfect example. We can let the white stripes on the flag remind us of that. Also, in Christ, we see that we have a way of having our sins forgiven. We can let the red stripes stand for the life he gave for us.

If we can look at the things in our flag in this way, then it can remind us of the basis for our nation. We are "One nation, under God." We are to be a nation of people who know that our blessings are gifts from God and we are called to respond to his love, as seen in the sacrifices of Jesus. Our response is to obediently follow the pure, holy, perfect example of our Lord, for this is the only way that leads to true, abundant life.

Possible Times To Use This Illustration In The Home:
- On a national holiday, when the flag is displayed.
- After watching a parade, in which the flag was carried.

The Cover

Purpose: To stress the importance of Bible reading.

Materials: A Bible with a black cover.

Lesson: Have you ever noticed that many Bibles have a black cover? I wonder why? It could be so that the dust of the room will not soil the cover since many people have the Bible set out on a table. I do not know the real reason behind the traditional black cover; but if you think about it for a moment, there is a good symbolic reason.

We say that the Bible contains the Word of God and that God's Word is a light unto our path. But the light cannot shine into our lives when the Bible remains closed. Therefore, a closed Bible, with its black cover, symbolizes spiritual darkness.

When we open the Bible, the pages appear to be very white, in contrast to the black cover. As we read God's Word in the scriptures, his light shines forth from the pages into our lives. A closed Bible is darkness; an open Bible means light for life.

Possible Times To Use This Illustration In The Home:
- When a child becomes indifferent to family devotions.
- When looking at the family Bible.
- To illustrate the importance of any kind of reading. The thoughts (light) from its pages cannot enter into our thinking until we open the book.

The Need For Balance

Purpose: To stress the need for a balanced life and for personal responsibility for it.

Materials: Two objects that you can balance on your hand. One should have a wide base. (A 4x4 that is several feet long will suffice.) The other can be a yardstick or a broom handle, or something like that. Practice with this narrower object so that you can get it to stand on your hand for at least a few seconds.

Lesson: Have you ever tried to balance something on your hand, like this stick? It is not easy to do. *(Show.)* You have to practice a lot. Now, if I try to balance something that has a wider base, it is easier. *(Show.)*

The same rule applies no matter what the shape of the object I am trying to balance. The rule is this: To balance it, you must have the same weight on all sides of the center. If you get too much on one side or the other, it will fall. *(Show this by slightly tilting your hand with the wide-based object on it.)*

As we look at the world around us, we see that there are many types of balances. How hot it would become if the sun were to shine all the time. The night balances the day and with the coming of darkness, we have a cooling effect. Think how many insects there would be if we had no birds or bats to help remove them. Many of the creatures of nature work to keep things in a proper balance so that we do not have too many of this or that.

We also need to see that our life is balanced. All work and no play can hurt life; and all play and no work is just as bad. Life is made up of many things, and we must be careful to keep all the parts of life in a proper balance. If we do not, then all life is affected by that part that is out of balance. For example, people who ignore the worship of God, who do not keep this experience as an active, real part of each week, soon find that the reality of God has disappeared from all of life. Jesus pointed to the need for balance when he said, "Man shall not live by bread alone." (Matthew 4:4)

Now, the working out of a proper balance between all the parts of a life is an individual matter. Just as I must hold my hand in the right position to balance this object, so each person must work with his or her own life to see that all things are in a proper relationship to all the other parts. Remember also that the best way to keep life balanced is to have God at the center of your life.

Possible Times To Use This Illustration In The Home:
- Upon returning home from a circus or other show where jugglers performed.
- When a child spends too much time watching television or in some other activity.

Listening To The Whistle

Purpose: To show the need to put into practice what we learn.

Materials: A whistle.

Lesson: There are many different kinds of whistles, but they all work in the same way. You take a deep breath and blow the air into the stem of the whistle, like this. *(Blow the whistle, but keep your finger over the top opening.)* What happened? No sound came forth from the whistle. Oh, I see. I had my finger over the opening here and, therefore, the air could not go through, no matter how hard I blew.

This shows us an important basic rule for the Christian life. God has given us many wonderful things. For example, we can study about Jesus and the things he taught. These truths pass into our life and make it better. But, like the air passing through the whistle, we must allow these teachings to pass through our life and be seen and heard by others if what we have received is to bring about the purpose for which God placed them within us.

Let me show you what I mean. What good does it do to know that God wants us to love our enemies if we never do it? What good does it do to know that we are not to steal or lie or cheat if we continue to do these things?

The Spirit of God must enter into us and be seen and heard in the way we live. Listen again to the whistle . . . and remember that if the outside force does not pass through, the whistle would be a useless instrument.

Possible Times To Use This Illustration In The Home:
- When a child fails to do what is expected.
- When a small child has just received a new toy whistle.
- After attending a game where a whistle was used by the referee.

Patience In Learning

Purpose: To remind children that patience is an essential part of life.

Materials: Building blocks, like those used by a small child. Enough small candy bars so that you can give one to each child.

Lesson: It probably has been some time since you played with blocks like these, but I imagine you still remember how to use them. I'd like each of you to take a block and let's see how high of a tower you can build together. *(Do so.)*

Now, let's think about what you had to do. You could only place one block on at a time, so you had to wait your turn. You had to be careful how you put your block on the one before yours so that the next block would have a good foundation. In order to be careful in placing your block, you had to take your time and do it just right. You see, building a tower with blocks takes a lot of patience.

The same thing applies to learning. You have to be patient as you learn. As a young child, first you had to learn how to stand up. Then you had to learn how to walk. After that, you learned how to run and play.

There are many people who become unhappy because they cannot do certain things. For example, a baby cannot play tennis while he is still an infant. First, he must learn to walk.

Then he has to learn how to run. Then he has to learn how to move about quickly and to coordinate his movements. Then he must learn how to swing the tennis racket and hit the ball. He must also learn the rules of the game. Finally, he must practice and practice and practice. Now, during all this time, the one who is learning must be patient. It may take many years before all the blocks, so to speak, are in place and he becomes a good tennis player.

You may feel that you are old enough to do something that someone else is doing, but then you are told that you must wait for one reason or another. When that happens, do not get angry; instead, be patient. Learn to do what you can do now and do it as well as you can. Then you will have a good foundation for doing other things later.

This morning I want to give you a little lesson in patience. Here is a candy bar. You may have it now, but I want you to wait until after lunch before you remove the wrapper and eat it.

Possible Times To Use This Illustration In The Home:
- When your child complains about not being able to do what an older brother or sister can do.
- When your child does not want to practice something that you feel is important for your child to learn.
- When you have been to a baseball game or a tennis match or some other event where practice and patience was needed by the players as they developed their skills.

How God Is Heard Today

Purpose: To help children understand one way whereby God speaks to people today.

Materials: A water goblet, made of thin glass. Fill about one-third full of water.

Special Preparation: Before making this presentation, practice producing a sound with the glass. Dip your finger in the water to moisten the tip of it. Then slowly run your finger — palm down — around the rim of the glass. Vary the pressure and speed until you produce a high pitched sound. A light touch works best.

Lesson: By rubbing your finger around the rim of this glass a vibration is set up in the wall of the glass. This sound is then amplified by the glass so that it can be heard. Let me show you what it sounds like.

One of the things we believe is that God speaks to people through other people. This singing glass helps us to see how it happens. Often people have an inner response to something they hear or see. They may read a passage of scripture, or hear a sermon, or see a special event. Whatever the cause, something happens to the person and he or she begins to vibrate in tune with God. When that happens, because God is with them, they represent God to the world around them.

51

When you feel like doing something good, or being kind or helpful, let this feeling, this vibration, find expression in your life. When you do this, you will be like the glass that receives a vibration at the edge and it is carried through the whole glass making the tone you hear. *(Make the glass sing again.)* As you respond to your good inner stirrings, it may be that God will be using you to present his word or his will to someone else.

Possible Times To Use This Illustration In The Home:
- At the dinner table.
- Another illustration can be presented by varying the level of water in the glass. This will change the sound and can be used to symbolize that the message of our life varies with the amount of faith and knowledge that we have.

The Spoiled Child

Purpose: To focus on one way that we learn from God.

Materials: A toy microscope.

Lesson: Do any of you have a toy like this? What is it? In many homes today, you can find this toy microscope. It is used to help children discover special facts. For example, it may be used to help a child see a small object, like an insect's wing, more clearly.

Now, there is one special feature of the microscope that you must remember. If you are to use a microscope you must look into it if you are to see what is there. No one can do it for you.

The same thing is often true in life. If parents do everything for a child, that child will never learn and will always expect others to do things for him or her. The result is what we call a spoiled child. Wise are the parents who let children do certain things, even when it would be easier for the parents to do those things themselves.

In this child-parent relationship, we learn a truth about our relationship with God. There are many things that God could do for us, but he does not; for he knows that the best way for us to learn is for us to do what we can for ourselves. If God did everything, we would become spoiled, ignorant children. We are expected to listen to God's instructions and to do what we can. Then, when more guidance is needed, we can turn to God in prayer.

Paul expressed this truth in these words, "Work out your own salvation with fear and trembling; for God is at work in you, both to will and to work for his good pleasure." (Philippians 2:12c-13) In other words, God is ever ready to help us; but we must be ready to do our part, working with him for the full abundant life. This does not mean that we work out our own plan and ignore God. Rather, desiring to do what is right in the sight of God, we work and God works and together we reach his goal which is for our good.

The child, through practice, learns to focus the microscope and to look into a new world of wonder. The Christian, through practice, learns to live life in God's world and with his fellow creatures in the way that God intended life to be lived.

Possible Times To Use This Illustration In The Home:
- When a child seems to expect others to do too much for him or her.
- When there is a need to show how we learn by doing things together, with each one doing his part, under the guidance of the one who knows more.

Using Your Imagination

Purpose: To encourage children to use their imagination for good.

Material: A toy airplane.

Lesson: How many of you have ever played with a toy airplane like this one? *(Wait for their answers.)* You can take such a toy and make believe that you are a pilot flying all around. You know, most of the joy that you receive in playing with toys comes from using your imagination. A girl may imagine that a doll is a real person, or a boy may think of his toy train as a real diesel engine, and so forth. It is wonderful to use your imagination.

However, we should not limit the use of our imagination just to those times when we are playing with toys. An active imagination can also guide us to do good things. Let me show you what I mean. Imagine how nice it would be in your classroom if everyone paid attention and no one disturbed the class. If you can picture how pleasant it would be, then you can be guided by that thought to do your part to make it that way. Imagine how wonderful it would be to have a lot of friends. This will encourage you to be more friendly to others. Imagine how happy your parents would be if you did what you know you should do, without being told to do it. Now seek to make that picture a reality by putting it into practice when you get home.

The imagination is a very powerful tool that you can use often. As you mature we hope that you will also learn to use your imagination for the good of others as well as for your own enjoyment.

Possible Times To Use This Illustration In The Home:
- When a child has been playing alone and has been using his or her imagination.
- When a child thinks of more mischief than good.

The Wind Sock

Purpose: To show that we need God's love and wisdom to give our lives proper direction.

Materials: A cloth in the form of a wind sock (miniature size).

Lesson: A wind sock, like this, is often used in a small airport to show in a general way, the force and direction of the wind. With this small make-believe wind sock, we can see how it works. Being inside, we can get the same effect of wind blowing by moving the wind sock around in the air. As I move it around in a circle, you can see the sock changing directions. Now, the stronger the wind, the higher the end will fly up. *(For a stronger wind, increase your speed of travel.)*

Our Christian life is like the wind sock. We can say that the wind sock shows us the nature of the wind as it blows through it. It shows us the direction of the wind and also gives us some idea of how strong or fast the wind is blowing. In a similar way, Christians show the nature of God as we allow his ways to flow through our lives, as we are driven by his Spirit and love.

Now it is important that the wind continue to flow through the sock if it is to be of any help to the pilots at the airport. If something blocks the wind then the wind sock will hang limp and lifeless. This is also true in the Christian life. If we are to show others what God is like then we must continue to let his wisdom and love guide us. And we must spend time learning about God so that his presence in our life will be strong. Regular Sunday worship and studying the Bible are two of the best ways to maintain our awareness of God and his love. Without the love of God flowing through our lives, they will become limp and lack direction, like this wind sock when no wind is flowing into it.

Possible Times To Use This Illustration In The Home:
- In the spring, when the March winds are blowing.
- In the summer, when your children think they should take a vacation from the worship of God.
- After a visit to an airport.

A Bucket Of Water

Purpose: To encourage children to actively seek the things of our faith.

Materials: A bucket half full of water.

Special Preparation: Hold the bucket at your side with your arm stiff and straight down. In a rapid circular motion swing the bucket to the front, up and over and down in the back. As the bucket reaches the downward position again, continue on around in the circular motion without stopping. Keep the bucket moving fast! When you wish to stop, be sure to stop in the position from which you started. Always make sure that the area around you is clear for the swing.

Lesson: I have put some water into this bucket. *(Let them look in to see it, or take a glass and fill it and then pour the water back from above the bucket so that the children can see that it contains water.)* Today I want to show you that it is possible to raise this bucket, over my head upside down, and have the water stay in the bucket. Of course, for this to happen, I have to handle the bucket of water in a very special way. Let me show you. *(Follow the above procedure.)*

The water stays in the bucket because of what we call centrifugal force. This force is set up whenever you move something rapidly around in a circle. The water in the bucket wants to fly out from the center as I spin it around in a circle. This force goes against the force of gravity when the bucket is over my head. Since the centrifugal force is greater than the pull of gravity, the water stays in the bucket and does not come down upon me.

There is a lesson here for us all. Life is continually subject to change. If we do not continue to grow, if we do not keep on moving forward; then we can easily lose what we have. During the summer vacation time, many children forget some of what they have learned simply because they do not use it. In time of sickness, we discover how weak our muscles become when we do not use them. When we have not worshiped God for a while, it seems that we have lost some of the feelings of his nearness.

To keep what we have we need to actively use it. This applies to the spiritual life as well as to the physical and mental parts of life. Jesus emphasized the need to keep growing when he said, "Seek and you will find." (Matthew 7:7) Our seeking for new knowledge and understanding is like the centrifugal force. As we move into the activity of seeking, doing so in relation to God who is the center of life, that which we need is forced into our life and becomes a real part of us.

Possible Times To Use This Illustration In The Home:
- When working in the garden and water is needed for the plants. Carry the water in a bucket and illustrate centrifugal force.
- During summer vacation, to encourage continuation of study and worship.
- To help a child understand the importance of actively seeking faith and knowledge with God at the center.

Learning From A Flower

Purpose: To show why we should be thankful to God.

Materials: A Bible and a flower that is growing in a pot.

Lesson: The first book of the Bible is named Genesis which means the beginning. We see why it has that name when we open the Bible and look at the first words. They tell us, "In the beginning God ...." The first story in the Bible goes on to tell us that God created this world and all that is in it. This is why we say that God has given us everything that we have.

We have so much that it is easy to take most of God's world for granted. For example, look at this flower. How beautiful it is. I think I will take it apart to get a closer look at it. *(Do so.)* This is very interesting. Now, I will put it back together again. Well, what do you know? I cannot do it. I have all the parts here, but no matter how hard I try — even if I use glue — I cannot put it together again so that it will continue to grow and remain beautiful.

You see, only God can make a flower; and this is just one little thing that God has made and given to us. We certainly have a lot for which we can thank God.

Possible Times To Use This Illustration In The Home:
- In the garden, when the family is enjoying the beauty of God's world.
- When a potted flower has been brought into the house; especially at a time of sickness, to remind the child of God's great gifts to us which includes the gift of medicine and healing.

A Disappearing Act

Purpose: It is not necessary to see God; but we can still experience God.

Materials: An electric fan and a paper straw.

Lesson: All of us have had many opportunities to see an electric fan in use. Because we have seen one in operation so often we may not have noticed the way the blades seem to disappear when they go around. *(Turn on the fan.)* We can see right through the fan because the blades are moving so fast that the eye cannot record each new position. In a sense, the blades are everywhere!

Perhaps this is one of the reasons why we cannot see God, for God is everywhere. But, as with the fan, so with God; the important thing is not the sight but the effect. We cannot see the blades of the fan when it is operating, but we feel the cooling breeze and we are thankful. Also, if an object enters the area of the blade's motion, we can hear and see what happens. *(Carefully place one end of the paper straw into the blades.)*

We cannot see God, but we hear and feel the effect of his presence in the world, and we are thankful. As we hear God's word, given to us in the Bible; and as we see the world he has made, we must not be disturbed by the fact that we cannot see him. Many of the important things in life cannot be seen. For example, we cannot see love, but we are aware of its presence. In regard to God, the Gospel of John tells us that "no one has ever seen God; the only Son ... he has made him known." (John 1:18)

Possible Times To Use This Illustration In The Home:
- In the summer, when a fan is being used.
- When a child asks to see God.

Hidden Treasure

Purpose: True life with God is like a great treasure.

Materials: A small chest or fancy box, and a bag of coins or play jewelry.

Lesson: Most boys and girls have imaginary adventures. Perhaps you have imagined that you were an explorer hunting for a lost treasure. How exciting it would be to dig up a container like this and open it and find a bag of money or jewels in it.

Jesus said that the Kingdom of God is like a treasure that has been hidden in a field and was found by a man. When he found it, he covered it up and then went and sold all that he had so that he could buy that field. In that way, the treasure became his and he was very happy. (cf. Matthew 13:44) What Jesus is telling us with this story is that living with God is so wonderful, so precious that it is of more value than everything else we have. In fact, it is of more value than all that we have!

Now, we learn to live with God by studying the Bible and by following the teachings of Jesus. The time that we give to this study is an investment in obtaining the great treasure of true life that God offers to all who will seek it. The great treasure is offered to us, but we have to accept it and claim it as our own. It is sort of like a treasure hunt that we enter into as long as we live. Jesus said, ''Do not lay up for yourselves treasures on earth, where moth and rust consume and where thieves break in and steal, but lay up for yourselves treasures in heaven, where neither moth nor rust consumes and where thieves do not break in and steal. For where your treasure is, there will your heart be also.'' (Matthew 6:19-21)

Possible Times To Use This Illustration In The Home:
- When the children have been playing imaginary games.
- When a child rebels against going to Sunday school.
- When there is need to emphasize what is important in life.

The Shortest Distance

Purpose: To encourage children to stick with a task until it is finished.

Materials: Two pencils or sticks and a piece of string; the ends of which are tied to the two sticks.

Lesson: With the help of these two pencils (or sticks) and this piece of string tied between them, we can see proof of the fact that the shortest distance between two points is a straight line. The length of the cord is fixed and as we hold the two points as far apart as possible, we see that a straight line is formed. If I move the two pencils (sticks) closer together, we see that we would go out of our way to get from one point to the other, if we follow the path of the string. We could walk farther than we need to if we followed the curved path. Or to put it another way: the shortest distance between two points is a straight line.

This is also an important lesson for life. When we apply it, we find that we can do a lot more. For example, when you set a goal before you remember that the shortest way to get to your goal and to get the job done is to go straight to the goal. When you start to offer excuses or you let other things take you from your task, then you are beating around the bush, you are curving away from your goal and it will take you longer to finish your task.

Boys and girls, when you have a job to do, like homework or washing the dishes, remember you will get through with your work in less time if you keep straight on the course, if you keep at it until you are done. Do not allow other things or thoughts to take you away from your path.

Possible Times To Use This Illustration In The Home:
- When a child procrastinates.
- When the family has been on a hike and has followed curving trails.
- When a child allows himself or herself to be distracted by many things.

Fine And False Speech

Purpose: To encourage children to tell the truth.

Materials: Two paper hats; one in the form of a crown and
the other in the form of the cone shape of a dunce cap.

Lesson: Here are two types of hats. Each one is worn by a
special person. This hat is called a dunce cap and when it is
worn it means that the person wearing it is not very smart.
This hat is a crown that is worn by a king to indicate that he
has power and wisdom.

Now, if you saw a person wearing this dunce cap *(Put it
on.)* you would not expect him to be able to teach you very
much. You would probably not pay too much attention to
whatever he said. On the other hand, if you saw a person wearing a real crown *(Put on the other hat.)* you would be attract-
ed to that person and you would expect words of wisdom to
be spoken by him.

A long time ago, a man discovered this truth and he wrote
in the Bible, "Fine speech is not becoming to a fool." That
is, you do not expect fine words to come forth from an ignorant person. "Fine speech is not becoming to a fool, still
less is false speech to a prince." (Proverbs 17:7) In other words,
we do not expect a noble person like a prince or a king to tell
lies.

Now, if we call God our Father, and we accept the fact that we are children of God, then the same thing can be said about us. God is like a great King; and if we are the children of God then we are princes and princesses. "Fine speech is not becoming to a fool, still less is false speech, or lies, or swearing, becoming to a child of God." You see, boys and girls, a Christian is expected to tell the truth. With our voices, we can say good things about God rather than to take his name in vain. Those who call God "Father" will want to do the right thing even with the way they talk.

Possible Times To Use This Illustration In The Home:
- When a child tells a lie or uses improper language.
- When a child is making things with paper.

The Rich And The Poor

Purpose: To encourage the children to be friendly to new children in the church.

Materials: An old suit coat that is patched.

Lesson: Most of the people that we see here today have nice clothes to wear. But what if someone, wearing this coat, came into your home or into our church? Would you greet them the same way as you would the boy who came with a new and expensive coat? You don't have to answer me. I just want you to think about what you would do.

James has given us some advice in regard to this type of situation. In the Bible, we hear him say, "Show no partiality." That means do not prefer one person over another. James says that you should show no partiality as you hold the faith of our Lord Jesus Christ, the Lord of glory. For if a man with gold rings and in fine clothing comes into your assembly, and a poor man in shabby clothing also comes in, and you pay more attention to the one who wears the fine clothing and say, "Have a seat here, please," while you say to the poor man, "stand here" or "sit at my feet" have you not made distinctions among yourselves, and become judges with evil thought? (James 2:1b-4)

In other words, all people are valued by God, not because of what they are or what they have; but simply because they are his creatures, his children. Now, if God would welcome them into his fellowship through Christ Jesus, should not we who carry the name of Christian extend the same welcome to all who come into our church home no matter who they are? From week to week, we never know who might enter into our church. When you meet a new boy or girl in church, remember the words of James. We are to treat all people the same. We are not to show preference for one person over another. Such actions on our part will help to make our church a warm and friendly place. Remember, boys and girls, it is just as important for you to do this when other children come into our church as it is for the adults to do it.

Possible Times To Use This Illustration In The Home:
- When your child makes fun of a poor person, or is unfriendly to someone of lesser means.
- To help a child realize that all people are precious to God.

The Jumping Flame

Purpose: To encourage children to try new things.

Materials: A candle and a few matches.

Special Preparation: Light the candle and then, with the lighted match near the candle flame and slightly above it, carefully blow out the candle flame. Do not blow out the match. Immediately, place the flame of the match into the smoke of the candlewick. Hold the match about one half an inch from the wick. If you do this quick enough, the flame will jump from the match and reignite the candle.

Lesson: Watch the flame on this candle very closely. This does not always work, but let me see if I can make the flame jump from the match to the candlewick. *(Try it. You may want to do it several times to be sure the children see what happens.)*

The lesson to be learned from this little experiment is something worth keeping in mind as long as you live. Very often, when we do not feel like doing something, when the flame of motivation dies down; we discover that when we force ourselves and enter into the activity, the flame of motivation returns. For example, you may not feel like going ice skating (or taking part in some other game, depending on the season), but someone keeps after you and brings their flame of motivation close to you and finally they talk you into going with them. Then once you are involved in the activity, most of the time, you will discover that you are glad that you decided to do it.

The same thing applies to your spiritual life. When you do not feel like going to church, or reading the Bible, or praying, force yourself to do it anyway. Enter into the activity that once had meaning for you and you will find that the flame of motivation will return. The Bible speaks of this in regard to God by telling us to "Draw near to God and he will draw near to you." (James 4:8a)

Possible Times To Use This Illustration In The Home:
- When a child does not feel like doing something and needs to be encouraged to try it.
- At the dinner table, when candles are part of the setting.
- This illustration can also be used to encourage children to share their enthusiasm with others.

A Lesson From Paper

Purpose: To help the children understand that as we grow older, we change; and we need to watch how we change.

Materials: A candle and several sheets of paper. On one piece of paper, write a word like Hello.

Lesson: A piece of paper is a very interesting object. You can fold it and it becomes a toy airplane that can fly. *(Do so.)* If you touch it to a flame, it turns into smoke and black ashes. *(Do so, carefully. You might want a metal container nearby into which you can drop the paper.)* You can write or print or draw on it and it becomes a source of communication. *(Show them your word paper.)*

In life, we are like a piece of paper. There are forces all around us that are trying to change us. Each day we grow a little older. Every time you allow someone to teach you something, whether it is your parents, your teacher, a friend or an enemy; you are changed. Sometimes the change is a good one and what you learn helps you to do something wonderful that you could not do before, like the paper being changed into an airplane. Other times, you learn something that is not good for you or for other people and the change may harm you or the people around you, like the way the paper was changed when the flame touched it. But no matter what the changes, let us remember that as we go through life, we carry a message that tells others what kind of person we are becoming. As Christians, we should want our lives to tell others about God's love and to show them what it means to believe in and follow Jesus.

As you go through life, look for good teachers that will change you for the better. Look for good friends that will bring out the best in you. Avoid those people who want to teach you harmful things. And remember always the good teacher that God has sent to help us all: Christ Jesus. Let him change you into a true child of God.

Possible Times To Use This Illustration In The Home:
- When a child picks up a bad habit from others.
- When a child loses his enthusiasm for learning.

The Arrow Of Friendship

Purpose: To think about the meaning of true friendship.

Material: One arrow. (The scripture reference for this is 1 Samuel 20.)

Lesson: Here is a modern day example of something that was used a long time ago to indicate one man's friendship for another person. Before David was the King of Israel, he had an enemy who wanted to kill him even though David wanted to be his friend. One of David's best friends was the son of this enemy. David wanted to come and talk to this man who did not like him, but he was not sure that it would be safe. So, his friend, Jonathan, said that he would let him know what things were like in his father's camp. This is how he would do it. David was to hide behind a certain rock near the camp. After Jonathan had discovered what kind of mood his father was in, he would let David know by shooting an arrow out into the field near the rock. Then he would send his servant after it. If it was safe for David to visit the camp, Jonathan would call to the servant, "You have gone too far, come towards me to find the arrow!" But if it was not safe, then he would call, "You have not gone far enough. Go away from me to find the arrow." Jonathan discovered that his father still wanted to kill David, and would do so on sight. So Jonathan used his arrow to send his friend, David, away to safety.

Friendship is one of the most valuable things we have. When you have a true friend, you should do all you can to help that friend. Jonathan helped David, not because he wanted to gain something for himself, but because he was his friend and he was in a position to help him.

In the family, all of us can help one another. In the family we can see clearly each other's needs. If we cannot be friends with the people in our own family, then how shall we be able to get along with others outside the family?

The head of the Christian family is King Jesus. The main law in his kingdom is the law of love. Therefore, the people of the Christian family should be the best of friends.

It has been said, that when we are in need, it is then that we find out who our true friends are; for a friend who helps another in the time of need is a true friend indeed.

Possible Times To Use This Illustration In The Home:
- When a child has had a fight with a friend.
- When a brother or sister refuses to help someone in the family when that person needs help.
- After members of the family have been out hunting.

Fishing With A Net

Purpose: To show the need for each one to accept responsibility for the total group experience.

Material: A fishing net.

Lesson: There are many ways to catch a fish. You can use a hook and line, or a spear, or even your hand, if you are fast enough. But the best way to catch a lot of fish at one time is to use a net like this. The net will cover a large area and will allow the water to go through, but will keep the fish within it.

Now, in a way, the people of our church are like a net that is seeking to catch others for Jesus. The church net is formed by all the people of the congregation as they work together. Even you boys and girls are part of that net. However, the net is only strong when everyone is willing to do their share and is willing to be a part of the total. Every time someone is absent, the net is made weaker. Each time a person is not friendly to a visitor in the church school class or in the sanctuary, then the net of love fails and there is a large hole and the stranger may slip away, perhaps never to be seen again.

Imagine what a large and effective net we would have if every member of our church were present every Sunday; especially if they came in the true Christian spirit of love and concern for others!

For the net to be strong, each one of us must see that we are doing our part in the right spirit. So, let us begin to build our net right now. Let me give you a hug and when you get back to your pew, give someone else a hug.

Possible Times To Use This Illustration In The Home:
- When the family has been out fishing.
- An application of this would be to talk about catching happiness in the home. Each person in the family must do his or her part, remembering that a Christian believes that true happiness comes from being able to give of yourself to others.

The Lever

Purpose: To show how people working together can accomplish more than the same number of people working alone.

Materials: Two poles, one shorter than the other.

Lesson: If you wanted to move a large rock you could do so by using a smaller rock and a pole. You would place the smaller rock near the large one and then use the pole as a lever. *(If you think the children are too young to understand this, show them a picture of a pole being used as a lever.)* I have two poles here. *(Show them to the children.)* One is shorter than the other. Which pole do you think would give you the most force to move the rock? If you were to experiment you would find that the longer pole would work better. In fact, the longer the pole or lever, the easier it is to move an object. The next time you have a big rock or a snowball to move, try it. However, if you plan to move a snowball, it will probably work better if you use a plank rather than a pole. The pole might cut into your snowball.

Now, as a family lives together, there are many times when there is work to be done. When one person works alone, it is very difficult to finish the task without using a lot of energy. But when all the members of the family work together, it is like having a longer pole or lever and the work is easier.

Try this experiment some night this week. After dinner, instead of running out to play or watching television, offer to help with the work of cleaning up the kitchen and see if the work is not easier for everyone. I am sure you will find that the family is happier during the evening hours because of your action. Then, what you learn to be true at dinner time, apply whenever there is work to be done that the whole family can do together.

Possible Times To Use This Illustration In The Home:
- In the winter when the children are making a snowman.
- After dinner, when everyone but mother has left the kitchen and the work is still to be done.
- Whenever there is a time when any member of the family fails to see the benefits of working together.

Useful Junk

Purpose: To show how God can refashion us into something good.

Material: Something that has been made out of scrap material and examples of the scrap used. (The lesson here is presented using a bowling pin lamp.)

Lesson: Here are two bowling pins. This one has been thrown out of the bowling alley, for it is too worn, as you can see. The other pin was also thrown away, for at one time it looked like the first pin. However, something happened to this second pin and now it is a useful lamp. *(Use a similar method to describe whatever remade object you might have.)*

Many people go through life and receive a number of hard blows and knocks and soon they feel like this old pin looks. *(Reword to fit your object.)* After a while, they begin to think that they are not good for anything anymore and in their own thinking they feel like a discarded pin in the game of life.

But other people, like this second pin, have learned that even after many hard blows, life can be made into something useful and beautiful. However, they had to learn that you cannot do it alone. The second pin, that looked like the first, became a lamp on a wood lathe and with a sharp tool and sandpaper reworking it and reshaping it.

God is the outside force that we need. He can cut away all that is ugly and useless. He can reshape us into that which he knows will be pleasing and useful.

Possible Times To Use This Illustration In The Home:
- After an accident or illness that limts someone in the family or who is known to the family.
- When a member of the family has made something beautiful and useful out of other material.
- When a child is discouraged with his or her limited abilities.

If The Shoe Fits

Purpose: To stress the importance of accepting help when it is needed.

Materials: Two shoes of obviously different sizes.

Lesson: This morning, before you came to church, you did something very important. I can see that you all did this important thing just by looking at you. You all put on a pair of shoes. But as I look at your shoes and at my shoes, I see that there are all sizes and kinds of shoes. One of the most important things about a pair of shoes is that they should fit. I could not wear your shoes and you would have a hard time walking very far in my shoes. As you can see, shoes are made in all sizes. Therefore, it is necessary that a person obtain ones that fit if they are to be suitable for wearing.

There is a saying that people will sometimes use about shoes that applies to many things. The saying is this: "If the shoe fits, put it on." What do you think that means? *(Let the children respond.)*

It means that if you hear something and it applies to you then it is up to you to take the wisdom or guidance of what was said and put it to work in your life.

This figure of speech also helps us to understand the right way to use guidance from other people. Shoes must fit so that they can be used, so that we can walk over rough surfaces or for long distances and not have our feet injured. Guidance is given for the same reason; namely, to help us move forward in life and endure the hardships, the rough spots on the road of life, and to protect us from harm.

When you hear words of guidance that you known contain useful information for you, put it on — take it to heart — and live with it. Living by some new idea, some new way of seeing life, may feel funny for a while, just like a new pair of shoes. But after those new shoes have been broken in by wearing them for a period of time, they feel more comfortable. So, also, with words of guidance. Once you accept them and live by them you will soon become comfortable with them.

For example, if someone says that people look better if they stand up straight and I accept that and then find myself walking around hunched over — when I remember that statement and I find that it applies to me; then I will stand straighter and look better. That is what it means to say, "If the shoe fits put it on." All the things that you learn in church and in school and at home are like this. When you hear something that seems right to you, then you have to apply it to your own life to make it true for you.

So now, you can use your shoes to carry you back to your parents and thank you for coming up here this morning.

Possible Times To Use This Illustration In The Home:
- When a young person needs guidance but will not accept it.
- When a new pair of shoes has been purchased, or old ones have become too small.

Let Your Light Shine Through

Purpose: To help children see that even little deeds of kindness are important.

Materials: A large piece of black cardboard or heavy paper and a sharp instrument like an ice pick, plus a floodlight.

Lesson: Behind this black paper is a light, but you cannot tell if the light is on or off, for none of the light is shining through. However, if I put a small hole in the paper, like this, you can see that the light is on. *(After a moment turn the light off.)*

In allowing the Christian faith to shine through our lives, our good deeds do not need to be big acts of love and concern. Even little deeds let some of the light of our faith shine into the lives of other people. This is especially true if no one else has shown concern for them for then there is a great deal of darkness in their life. If that is the case, then our little light will shine very bright and it will make life better for them.

Now, one of the little deeds of concern that even a little child can do is the deed of friendliness. When you see another person do you take time to say "Hello?" I have seen so many boys and girls who do not even say hello to someone when that person greets them.

When you greet someone, especially if it is with a smile, it is like turning the light on. *(Turn on the floodlight again.)* With each greeting a little light shines through the darkness and into the hearts of others and it will make our world a little bit better.

When each Christian does his or her part, we find that all the little lights coming together form a brilliance that will glorify God who is the source of our true light in life. *(As you speak, remove the paper from in front of the light. Do not let the floodlight shine into the eyes of the little children, especially if it is extremely bright. Point it upward or away from them.)*

Possible Times To Use This Illustration In The Home:
- When floodlights are being used to take a picture or to show off your outside house decorations at Christmas time.
- When a young person seems to be growing weary of doing good deeds, feeling that his or her little contribution will not make any difference.

Try, Try Again

Purpose: To encourage children to keep on trying when they have difficulty doing anything.

Material: No special material is needed. The little song, used here, has finger movements to use with it. If you know them, they can be used.

Lesson: Do any of you know the little song "The Itsy Bitsy Spider?" Let's do it together. It goes like this:

The itsy bitsy spider went up the water spout.
Down came the rain and drove the spider out.
Out came the sun and dried up all the rain.
And the itsy bitsy spider went up the spout again."
(Author unknown)

That little song has a very important lesson for us all. What do you think it might be? *(Give time for an answer.)* To me, this song says, if at first you don't succeed, try, try again. When the water knocked the spider down, he did not stay down, but climbed up again.

This is something that we all need to remember in life. If we have difficulty doing something then we need to remember this little spider. If we fail, we should try again and again. We must not let a difficult time stop us from moving on to better things.

89

Possible Times To Use This Illustration In The Home:
- When you see a spider.
- During a rainstorm.
- When your child gives up too easily.

The Pretzel

Purpose: To think with the children about stewardship and prayer.

Material: A bag of pretzels.

Lesson: Somewhere I read that pretzels were created by a monk who lived in Southern France about the year 610. The purpose of the pretzel was to use up some of the scraps of dough that were left after his baking chores were over. In this way every bit of material was used so that nothing would be wasted. He formed the shape of the pretzel to represent the arms of children folded in prayer. To put these little loops of baked dough to good use, he began to give them to children as a reward for learning their prayers. In fact, the lowly pretzel came to be a symbol for excellence in many activities. *(Note the symbol for the Olympic games.)*

This is just one illustration of the way that our Christian faith has influenced all of life. But more than that, it reminds us of the place of prayer in the ordinary affairs of every day. You see, you can give thought to prayer anywhere, in the heat of a kitchen as well as in the cool of the garden or in the beautiful setting of the church. The symbol of children at prayer, the pretzel, speaks to us of the simple love and trust that are at the heart of all true prayers.

The pretzel also helps us to remember that we are not to waste things. That is good stewardship. Also, we are to use whatever we have to the honor and glory of God. Do the best you can with whatever you have no matter how little it may seem to be.

Since the first pretzels were used as a reward to children, today each one of you can have a pretzel as a reward for coming up here. Thank you.

Possible Times To Use This Illustration In The Home:
- When a child has wasted good material by throwing it away when some of it could have been salvaged.
- When eating pretzels.
- When you want to give a child a simple reward for a job well done.

On Using Problems

Purpose: To think about the reason for problems in life.

Materials: A large rubber ball, or basketball. Pieces of round candy to give to the children.

Lesson: I want you to watch this ball. *(Throw it into the air several times.)* With your eyes open, you can tell what I am doing. Now, close your eyes and see if you can tell what I am doing. Since you cannot see the ball you must rely on your ears to tell you what is happening. And the only time they will help you is when the ball is bounced off the floor, like this. You may open your eyes. The only time you can tell what is happening when your eyes were closed was when the ball ran into trouble; when it bounced off of something and had to change its course.

So also in life. Often the only time others can tell what is happening to you on the inside, where no one can see, is to listen to you when you run into trouble. If you cry every time things do not go your way, the sound says, "This person is selfish." If you speak of revenge and getting even when someone causes you trouble, that says, "This person has not learned how to forgive."

I think one of the reasons we have problems in life is so that we and others can understand what we are like on the inside, in our heart and mind and soul. If Jesus lives with us and in us, people will hear the effect of his presence as we run into the problems of life. Remember also that our faith can help us to know how to respond to our problems.

Your parents learned a long time ago to not only look at you but to listen to you as well. They can tell how you feel by the way you sound. And the same thing is true for you. If you listen to your friends or your brother or sister, or even your parents, you can tell when they are unhappy or having a problem and if you try, maybe you can help them feel better.

One of the important lessons of life is to be willing to listen to other people so that you know how they feel and to help them when you can.

Now, I can't give each one of you a ball to play with; but I can give you a malt ball (or some other kind of round candy) to enjoy as a reminder of what we talked about today.

Possible Times To Use This Illustration In The Home:
- When a child is having difficulties and refuses to talk about them.
- When a child expresses anger too quickly and then is sorry for what has been said. We need to help children learn self-control. It is not good enough to be sorry for the misuse of problem times, we must learn from them and allow others to help us to a better way of life.

Zero

Purpose: Learning to handle failure.

Material: Make a large zero out of cardboard and color it black.

Lesson: Now and then, we receive this mark for our efforts. *(Hold up the zero.)* We fail a test or we strike out at a baseball game, or we miss the mark in one way or another. What should we do when we get a zero? We should ask ourselves a number of questions.

First, we should ask: "Did I do the best I could? Did I take advantage of the time I had to prepare myself as best I could; or was I lazy? To avoid zeros we need to use our time wisely. We need to prepare ourselves for what we know is coming.

Secondly, if you did the best you could and still received a zero, what does that say to you? It says: "No one is perfect. We all miss the mark in some area of life. No one can excel in everything." It may be hard to admit to yourself that you are not perfect, but it can also be a rewarding experience. It can help us come closer to God who will guide us as we seek to make life better.

Finally, we must ask: "Does this zero disturb me because of what others might think about me for receiving it?" If you have done your best, God will know and that is all that really matters. As Paul pointed out, the Christian is to do good as unto God and not unto other people. (cf. Ephesians 6:7) When we remember that, we will seek to give God our best at all times. We are expected to do the best we can, but we need not be the best in whatever we do.

Possible Times To Use This Illustration In The Home:
- When a child fails in something or does not win the top prize.
- When a child blames someone else or something other than self for a failure.
- When a child is overly concerned about what others might think of him or her.

Symbols Of Thanksgiving
— Stone And Rope

Purpose: To stress our need to thank God for all the good things that have come to us in life.

Materials: A large stone that you can hold in the palm of your hand and a piece of rope, about two feet long.

Lesson: It is very important to understand what a symbol stands for. Here is a stone and a piece of rope that are symbols of thanksgiving. But to understand their symbolism, we need to know about a practice from Old Testament times. Long ago in Palestine, farmland was given to village families each year by lot. Let me tell you what that meant. At the beginning of the planting season, small stones were marked with numbers. Each family had a different number and each stone had just one number on it. These stones were placed in a bag and a little child was chosen to draw them out, one by one. The first number drawn would get the best land. After each family had been allotted its section of land, they would measure it with a line and mark its boundaries with stones. If a family had good fortune, their lot and their measuring line would give them good land upon which to plant the crops for that year. Good land meant a good harvest and for that they were thankful.

King David expressed his gratitude for what God had done for him in terms of the stone or lot and the rope or line. He said, "The Lord is my chosen portion and my cup; thou holdest my lot. The lines have fallen for me in pleasant places; yea, I have a goodly heritage." (Psalm 16:5, 6)

In our country, we have had much good fortune. We live in pleasant places. God has given us so much. We too must learn to be willing to say "Thank you" to God for all that he has given to us.

Possible Times To Use This Illustration In The Home:
- When planting a garden.
- During or after a vacation trip when you have seen the beauty of America.
- At the Thanksgiving season.
- After a visit to a farm.

The Wishbone

Purpose: How to reach our goals in life.

Material: A chicken or turkey wishbone.

Lesson: As you probably know, this is called a wishbone. Most children like to take hold of it and make a wish and then break it apart. The one who gets the biggest piece is supposed to have their wish come true. I'm sure all of us can think of many things that we would like to have in life and sometimes we do obtain what we want. However, one of the best ways to reach your goal, whatever it might be, is not to break a wishbone and then expect your goal to be granted to you as if by magic. Breaking a wishbone is fun, but it is not a very realistic approach to life.

Paul knew the right way to reach a goal. He saw the goals that were set before him by the example of Jesus, and then Paul said, "Not that I have already obtained this or am already perfect, but I press on to make it my own, because Christ Jesus has made me his own .... Forgetting what lies behind and straining forward to what lies ahead, I press on toward the goal for the prize of the upward call of God in Christ Jesus." (Philippians 3:12, 13b-14) Paul knew what he wanted in life. He knew what his goals were, and he pressed on, straining and working hard to reach them. He did not just sit back, or even break a wishbone, and say, "Oh, I wish for this ...."

Instead of just wishing and doing nothing, he worked hard and long to obtain his goal, even though the goal was one he could not fully reach in this life.

The principle is true for all of us: the best way to make your dreams come true is to work hard and long; to press on and push forward and not to be held back by the past.

Possible Times To Use This Illustration In The Home:
- When you have a wishbone to be broken.
- When a child keeps wishing for something, but does nothing to try to obtain that goal.

What Shall You Give?

Purpose: To share with the children some wonderful gifts they can give to their parents.

Materials: Several boxes wrapped like Christmas or birthday presents.

Lesson: There are several times during the year when children think about presents, like these. I imagine that all of you give thought to gifts at Christmas time. Then, when your birthday draws near, I am sure that again you begin to think about what you might like to receive. But for a few moments today, I'd like you to think about what you can give to others on their special day; especially to your parents.

How would you like to give them something that would cost no money, yet it would be a priceless gift that only you can give? And because you give it, it will mean a great deal to your mother or father.

Let me suggest a few of these priceless, wonderful gifts. I am sure that you will be able to think of others. One is the gift of affection and you can give it by saying, "I love you Mom and Dad!" It is a gift that only you can give. In a birthday card, that you could make yourself, you could tell them that you love them. Then plan to follow up by telling them those same words every day.

Another gift is the gift of appreciation, of saying, "Thank you," not only when you receive a gift like this *(Hold up a package)*, but all through the year whenever they give you something or do something special for you. Again, in your birthday card to them, you can write a thank you note and then follow up with words of thank you each day after that.

Another wonderful gift for your mother and father is that of being kind to your brothers and sisters, or to your friends when they are in your home. This is a wonderful gift, for it brings peace and harmony into a family. It creates the conditions that enable people to be happy and makes your home a place where people like to come. Again, in a birthday card, you can tell your parents that your gift to them will be to show more kindness to others.

There are many such gifts that you can give to your parents and to others in the home. All you have to do is to keep your eyes and ears and heart open and you will discover what you can give. And in giving, you will receive in return the ingredients of happiness.

Possible Times To Use This Illustration In The Home:
- At Christmas time or when a birthday is approaching.
- On any occasion, when your child seems to be too interested in what gifts might be received.

A Winter Experiment

Purpose: To think about how love affects us all.

Materials: A large piece of ice. A thin strong wire and two heavy weights that can be attached to the wire. A dish pan to hold the ice.

Special Preparation: Tie the weights on the ends of the wire. Place the wire over the ice. Make sure that the weights hang free so that they can move downward as the wire cuts through the ice. Start the procedure before you plan to use it.

Lesson: This piece of wire was placed over the ice about one hour ago. As you can see, the wire has slowly melted the ice and is cutting into it. The ice under the wire is melting quicker because of the heat of compression. If you press your thumb and finger together, as hard as you can, you should feel an increase in warmth there. This also is heat caused by compression.

Love, that is expressed in the form of kindness, good will and concern, is like the weighted wire. Love is a force that can cut through the icy spirit or the hard of heart. Love will add the warmth that is needed in every life. Often, however, it takes a long time before we see the effects of true love. But even though the process is slow, we must believe, with Paul, that love never ends. (cf. 1 Corinthians 13:8) Love, constantly applied, like the compression of the wire on the ice, will produce a wonderful warmth in life.

Possible Times To Use This Illustration In The Home:
- The best time to conduct this experiment is in the winter when the ice will not melt too quickly.
- A good time to use it, as the beginning of a conversation in the home, would be during or after a winter ice storm, or after the family has been ice skating. You might place the weighted wire over a large piece of ice to let it cut through while you are away. Then observe the effect when you return. (Note: You might also notice the way ice skating melts the ice when people skate upon it. Again, it is the warmth of compression that accounts for this melting.)
- After you have been to an ice skating show, or watched ice skating on television.

New Year's Resolution

Purpose: To remember that outward appearances are not the most important things in life.

Materials: Three small jars containing salt, sugar and flour respectively.

Lesson: I have here three jars and, as you can see, each contains something white. From a distance, they all look alike; but if you were to put them to the use for which they were intended, you would see that they are very different.

This is salt and you might use it on your breakfast eggs. But you would not use this on eggs, for this is sugar. However, you might use it at breakfast on cereal. The third white substance would not be used on either eggs or cereal for it is flour. But you might have a piece of bread at breakfast that is made with flour.

All three ingredients look alike and can even be used at the same meal, but they are different. You see, it is not the outward appearance that makes things what they are. It is the special inner qualities that they possess that determines how they are used.

Jesus said that we are the salt of the earth, but if the salt has lost its saltiness, it is good for nothing and can be thrown away. (cf Matthew 5:13) God has placed us in this world and he expects us to live in a certain way and by doing so we maintain our saltiness, so to speak; for we use life in the right way for the right purpose.

The beginning of a new year is a good time for you to look at yourself, and to think about the kind of qualities you want in your life. Let me suggest a few of these qualities that the Bible says are important for us to have: Patience, kindness, love and self-control are some of the inner characteristics that everyone needs to live as God intended us to live.

Possible Times To Use This Illustration In The Home:
- At the breakfast table (especially on New Year's Day).
- When looking upon a winter scene and recalling other things that are white.
- When making bread.

Earphones

Purpose: To share with the children our need for time alone and time with other people.

Materials: A portable radio, like a Walkman and earphones.

Lesson: I have several things I want to show you this morning. First, what is this? . . . (a radio) What do you do with a radio? . . . (listen) Now, what is this? . . . (earphones) Have any of you ever used earphones? . . . What are they used for? . . . (to listen)

(Turn on the radio.) An interesting thing happens when I plug in the earphones. *(Show.)* The sound no longer comes from the speaker in the radio, but just from the earphones. *(Let one or two children listen to confirm your statement.)*

Why would you use earphones when you can listen to a radio over the speaker? . . . (to not disturb others) This reminds us of two very important things about life.

First, there are times when it is right to do something all by yourself. It is your own private activity and it does not need to be shared with others. You need to remember this for other people also. Sometimes your mother or father or your brother or sister may want to be alone; and the earphones are a symbol of the need we all have for private time.

The second thing we learn from the earphones and the radio is that there are times when we need to pull the plug so

107

that everyone can hear and enjoy the music or whatever the event might be. Life is not just being alone, it is also doing things with others.

Learning when to share and when to be alone is very important, for we all need time together and time apart. It is something we all need to work at. I hope you will remember that whenever you see or use earphones.

Possible Times To Use This Illustration In The Home:
- When a child is spending too much time alone.
- When your child is not willing to let other members of the household have any time alone.
- When a child has difficulty sharing.

Even Children
Can Be Good Samaritans

Purpose: To encourage children to be good Samaritans.

Material: No special material is needed.

Lesson: Today I would like you to help me tell a story. There was a little boy who came to *(Name your city or town.)* to visit his grandparents. He had never been here before. Then one day, he decided to take a walk, all by himself, to look around this new place. After a while, he discovered that he was lost. He did not know how to get back to his grandparents' home. All he could do was to stand on a corner and cry.

Now, in our story, you see the little boy crying. What would you do? ... If you offer to take him home, but he says, "I am not supposed to go with a stranger," what would you do? ... (Go home and call his grandparents; and if he does not know their last name, call the police.) If you have someone with you, maybe that person could stay with the little boy to comfort him until help arrives.

This is just a story, but you never know when you might be able to help someone, if you are willing to do so. Keep your eyes open wherever you are and if you see a person in need of help, and you think you can help them, check it out and see what you can do. Even children can be good Samaritans. It is part of what it means to be a Christian.

Possible Times To Use This Illustration In The Home:
- When your child needs a boost in self-confidence.
- When you are trying to help your child understand when and when not to talk to strangers.
- You might turn the exercise around and ask your child what he or she would do if they were lost like the little boy. Children need to think about possible experiences so that they will be prepared if they have a need.

Silence

Purpose: Learning to use silence.

Materials: Homemade cookies to share.

Lesson: This morning I want you to try to find something. It is always here, but it can be easily lost. It can be lost by our own actions, but it requires the help of others to find it. Let us see if we can find it together. Do you know what we are looking for? ... It is almost here. There it is. SILENCE. *(Do not say anything for a period of time.)* We seldom have complete silence for there is almost always some sounds being made around us.

Now, what do you think a person can do with silence? ... *(If there is no response, wait a moment and say:)* You are doing it right now. Silence is a good time to think for yourself. And thinking is necessary if you are to do good things for other people.

If I ask you for a glass of water when I am thirsty and you get it for me, you are just responding to the sounds I have made. But if you think I might be thirsty, and you offer me a glass of water before I ask for it, then you are showing love and concern. You are thinking for yourself.

Now, I think I would like to show my love for you today. So, I think I will give you all a little gift. It is a gift that I have made myself, just for you. I hope you will enjoy these homemade cookies.

Possible Times To Use This Illustration In The Home:
- When a child needs to be encouraged to take the initiative to do something good for other people.
- When you have made cookies at home.
- When your child seldom lives in an environment of silence.

Easter Is Colorful

Purpose: To remind the children that life is beautiful with Jesus and because of Jesus.

Materials: Easter lilies and/or Easter eggs, plus some small colored candy eggs to hand out.

Lesson: This morning I want you to think with me about what we see on this day that we call Easter. Let's look around and you tell me what you see that we do not always see in church ... *(If the children do not respond, tell them what you see.)* First, notice the beautiful white lilies with the touch of yellow in the center and the dark green paper around the base. Next, look at the people out there, all dressed up in their Easter clothing. Did you have anything special at home this morning? Maybe you found some Easter eggs that have been colored with bright colors. Everywhere we look we see colorful and beautiful things today. This reminds us of part of the meaning of this day. Easter celebrates life and living. In Jesus, we are offered a bright and beautiful life. We have so much to be thankful for because of Jesus.

This morning I would like to give each one of you a little reminder of what Easter means. This day should fill us all with great happiness. *(Give colored candy eggs.)*

113

Possible Times To Use This Illustration In The Home:
- On Easter or any time during the spring.
- When a child needs to be reminded of the beauty of the Christian faith.

Index

AUBURN HILLS PRESBYTERIAN CHURCH

DATE DUE
